DEDICATION

This book is dedicated to job seekers everywhere who believe in themselves and are willing to go for it ALL THE WAY!

1

GETTING HIRED IN THE '90s

Everything You Always Wanted To Know About Finding A Job But Were Afraid To Ask

FIRST EDITION
Edited by Darcy Westcott
Cover Design, **Stevens Design,** Schaumburg, IL
Library of Congress **Cataloging in Publication Data**
Spina, Vicki L. 1958-
        Getting hired in the '90s everything you alway wanted to know about finding a job but were afraid to ask / Vicki L. Spina
        p. cm.
        Includes Index.
        ISBN 0-9633287-0-0

        1. Job hunting. 2. Employment interviewing. I. Title. II.
Title: Getting hired in the nineties. III. Title: Everything you
always wanted to know aobut finding a job but were afraid to ask.

HF5382. 7. s65 1992   658.14
                        QBI92-20060

ATTENTION SCHOOLS & CORPORATIONS ! GETTING HIRED IN THE '90s is available at quantity discounts with bulk purchase for educational or business use.

GETTING HIRED IN THE '90s

Everything You Always Wanted To Know About Finding A Job But Were Afraid To Ask

GETTING HIRED IN THE '90s includes HUNDREDS OF IDEAS for today's job seeker. This book covers everything from: preparing to interview effectively...writing a great cover letter and resume...uncovering the hidden job market... handling tough interview questions...success stories.. negotiating the offer and finally, STARTING A NEW JOB !

ACKNOWLEDGEMENTS

I would like to take this opportunity to **thank several individuals.** Without their help and support, this book would not be possible.

Above all I thank GOD. His love guides me through life and comforts me every moment of each day.

Anita Kurz who took a chance on hiring me in the employment business. Thank you for recognizing my potential and for being my teacher.

Cheryl Miller who has no idea that it was after meeting and interviewing her that I decided to write this book. Thank you for your inspiration.

Scott Waldner who helped me face my fear and realize what I have to say is important!

Jill Halper who's unyielding belief, friendship and honesty gave me the confidence to finish. Thank you my dear friend.

Kathleen Dense who from the moment I started this project was so excited and proud of me. Her support and love helped me to believe in myself. Thank you.

Christine Veome who's exceptional gift of phrasing and terminology added the finishing touches.

Karen Kennedy who's excellent word processing skills and her ability to take all my scribbles and put it all together helped make my dream a reality.

Darcy Westcott who's attention to detail and superb editing ability created the professional image I desired.

Laurie Zipnick who came into my life when I needed a friend and gave me her total love and support.

Sean Flynn who was my gift from GOD. Without his complete faith and dedication to this project, this book would not have been possible. Thank you.

Nancy Johnson who is the best Mother in the world. Your unconditional love has always made me feel safe and strong. Thank you for always being there for me. I Love You.

And last but not least, my daughters **Carli and Caitlyn.** Their energy and excitement for life continually give me the incentive to keep forging ahead. Thank you for teaching me that dreams do come true! I Love You both from the bottom of my heart.

WHAT PEOPLE ARE SAYING.....

..... *It's straight to the point, comprehensive and easy to understand, short enough that each chapter will keep the reader involved and intense about the subject matter, as well as being the absolute and most perfect advice that you could be offering people, not only today, but for all times.*

> *Alan R. Schonberg*
> *President*
> *MANAGEMENT RECRUITERS INT'L*

..... *I received over more than 300 resumes for a recent opening in our company. The individual I hired was not the most qualified, but definitely the best prepared. It wasn't only how he answered my questions, it was the questions he asked me that made me decide on hiring him. I strongly recommend GETTING HIRED IN THE '90s to any candidate that wants to knock an employer's socks off- mine were!*

> *Mr. Michael Harper*
> *Sales Manager, Skytel Corporation*

..... *I had always felt that I interviewed well. Reading your book gave me the extra edge I needed! Thanks to GETTING HIRED IN THE '90s I am now with a company I absolutely love!*

> *Joy McCaffrey*
> *Marketing Sales Support Representative*

..... *A brilliant tool for any individual looking to find another position. Due to my reading GETTING HIRED IN THE '90s I was selected from over several hundred applicants. I am fortunate that I had the opportunity to read this book!*

> *Gregory Hay*
> *Account Executive, Skytel Corporation*

..... *Thank you for writing one of the finest job search books I've seen. It is comprehensive and easy to apply. I know it will be a SMASHING BESTSELLER!*

> *Mr. Stephen Resch*
> *Director of Placement*
> *PURDUE UNIVERSITY*

CONTENTS

INTRODUCTION

Are you frustrated, bored and underpaid at your current job? Not getting the recognition or promotions you deserve? Maybe you are one of thousands that lost your job due to lay-offs or perhaps you have recently graduated from school and need direction? Are you angry at the current lack of jobs available, feeling scared, alone and isolated? Thought that being out of a job would never happen to you? IF YOU HAVE ANSWERED YES TO ANY OF THESE QUESTIONS, TAKE HEART! <u>THIS BOOK WILL HELP YOU SORT OUT YOUR FEELINGS, PREPARE FOR YOUR JOB SEARCH AND GIVE YOU THE GUIDANCE AND CONFIDENCE TO GET WHERE YOU WANT TO GO IN YOUR CAREER.</u>

Chances are, you were unprepared when you interviewed for your current or last position. You probably did not know the right questions to ask. Don't feel bad. **Most people do not know how to interview effectively because they were never taught how.**

Spina comments, "When I graduated from school I knew the basics of finding a job. First, contact the want ads and try to get an interview. Next, hope I was qualified. When I was actually called in for an appointment, I was usually too nervous and unprepared to make a great impression. I thought if I was really lucky I might get a job offer. Little did I know, **I had a lot more control over getting hired than I thought!"**

Vicki L. Spina started her successful career in personnel placement in 1979. During the last 13 years she has had the opportunity to work with thousands of candidates and employers. Through her <u>extensive interviewing</u> and employer contact, she has **developed** and **taught unique and successful interviewing techniques that get results!** Spina's career

success depends on her ability to coach candidates on presenting themselves in the strongest possible way to receive a job offer. **More than 75% of the candidates she prepares for an interview receive an offer by their second interview.**

In 1980, her rookie year, Spina was recognized as the **Nation's** number two **Account Executive of the Year**, surpassing counselors who had been in the employment business for years.

Consistently ranked among the top counselors in her field, she is often asked what her secret is. Spina sums it up in five words: "I am a good listener."

By listening to feedback from thousands of employers she is able to determine who they hire and why. **Spina has also discovered that the most qualified person does not always get hired. The one who is best prepared does! This is why she has decided to share with you all the success stories and interviewing tips she has learned throughout the years.**

The unique information in this book will provide **easy step by step instructions** on everything from preparing to interview effectively, writing an attention-getting resume and cover letter, interviewing confidently, following up after the interview and finally **GETTING THE JOB OFFER YOU WANT!**

So, if you are confused about looking for a new job or need to fine tune your interviewing skills nineties style...READ ON!.

chapter one

Should you Be Interviewing?

SHOULD YOU BE INTERVIEWING?

Do you have a difficult time getting up for work and when you finally get there, do you constantly look at your watch waiting for 5:00 o'clock to roll around?

If so, then it is time to take stock of your current position. **Take a few minutes to complete the following questionnaire** which will show how satisfied you are with your present situation. For those of you who are not currently employed, I suggest you **complete the following questions with your last position in mind**.

QUESTION	YES	NO
1. Do you enjoy your job responsibilities at least 75% of the time?		
2. Do you have a good working relationship with your boss and co-workers?		
3. Are you paid a fair wage for your position and responsibilities?		
4. Are advancement opportunities available to you in the near future?		
5. Are you recognized and respected for your contributions?		
6. Are you challenged by your position and learning new skills?		
7. Have you been overlooked for a promotion more than once?		
8. Are you satisfied with your position and feel good about yourself?		
9. Are you proud of your position and career accomplishments?		
10. Does your position allow you time for a personal life?		

If **you answered No** to three or more of these questions, **start preparing for your job search.** It may be that you do not have to look outside your present company (unless you answered Yes to question seven). Your company may have an internal job posting system. I suggest you start by investigating those possibilities first. If you choose to remain at your current company, you need to ask your direct supervisor to review your job performance. Make sure you have a private office to talk with uninterrupted time. Prepare a list of the reasons why you should be promoted and given a raise. Express your concerns in a calm manner. DO NOT threaten to leave if you do not get your way.

After your meeting if you are not satisfied with the results, turn to Chapter Two.

Remember, good communication with your current boss is essential if you plan to remain in your current position or move up within a corporation. Do not make a hasty decision if the promises your company makes do not occur immediately. Give the deal about 90 days to come to fruition and if the situation does not improve, read Chapter Two.

> **TIP:** It is wise to always have an updated resume on file. **The best time to look for a new job is when you are currently employed and happy with your position.** Your self-esteem is at its highest and you are not desperate to leave.

A **positive self-image is a very important** part of the interviewing process. If you have recently been fired or have been out of a job for a while, the following philosophy is especially crucial to your success in finding a new position. Ask yourself, **"Why should a company hire me?"** or **"If I were the owner of the company, would I hire myself?"**

If you cannot list at least five solid reasons for a company to hire you, then you need to work on your self-image. Following is a partial list of qualities companies look for. **Circle the words that describe your best traits.**

Anticipate Boss's Needs	Honest
Cooperative	Independent
Dependable	Initiative
Detail Oriented	Intelligent
Efficient	Positive Attitude (Enthusiastic)
Flexible	Problem Solver
Good Communication Skills	Professional
Good Follow Up Skills	Quick Learner
Healthy	Team Player

If you are suffering from ill health or personal problems, the timing may not be right for a job search. **A successful job search requires energy, enthusiasm and a positive attitude to convince the employer you are the ideal individual for the position.**

Concentrate on getting back on your feet emotionally and physically before starting your job search. **The following motivational and inspirational tapes and books are recommended for the emotional side of your job search:**

"The Power of Positive Thinking" by Norman Vincent Peale

"How To Be A No-Limit Person" by Dr. Wayne Dyer (Available in audio-tape)

"How To Win Friends And Influence People" by Dale Carnegie

"What To Say When You Talk To Your Self" by Shad Helmsetter, Ph.D

"Return To Love" by Marianne Williamson (Available in audio-tape and book)

Before you continue on to Chapter 2, **have you taken the action necessary** to get off to **the best possible start?** Have you skipped over one of the most important aspects of a successful job search? **YOUR ATTITUDE!** Keep an open mind and **take action** on the suggestions offered while you are reading this book and you will be rewarded with **reaching your goal of finding a new position quickly and easily.**

TIP: A great deal of negativity and rejection exists when looking for a new job. I suggest you fill your mind with as many positive affirmations as possible to alleviate negative feelings you may be experiencing.

chapter two

PREPARING To INTERVIEW EFFECTIVELY

PREPARING TO INTERVIEW

In order to best prepare for the interview, you must know yourself first. After all, you are the subject at hand.

First, identify and list your five likes and dislikes. (See worksheet below.)

EXAMPLE:

LIKES	STRENGTHS	DISLIKES	WEAKNESSES
Computers	Detail Oriented/ Technical Aptitude	Figure Work	Math
Fast Paced Environment	Works Well Under Pressure	Writing Business Letters	Written Communication Skills
People Contact	Sales/Customer Service	Meeting New People	Shyness

	LIKES	STRENGTHS	DISLIKES	WEAKNESSES
1.				
2.				
3.				
4.				
5.				
6.				
7.				
8.				
9.				
10.				

NOTE: Your likes and dislikes may reflect what your strengths and weaknesses are.

Next, outline three of your special talents and achievements.

EXAMPLE

TALENTS	ACHIEVEMENTS
Creative, award-winning ideas	Designed innovative company logo
Flair for selling	Developed substantial client following
Great rapport with customers	Ranked in top 5% nationwide (1989 - 1991)

TALENTS	ACHIEVEMENTS
1.	
2.	
3.	
4.	
5.	
6.	

Use the following section as your worksheet to determine your personal career direction (your interests and qualifications). Included are breakdowns of different positions available as well as industries in which positions exist. **Check off as many of the categories that apply to you.**

ACCOUNTING					
Accountant (Cost)		Billing		Payroll	
Accountant (Tax)		Bookkeeper		Supervisor/Manager	
Accounts Payable/Receivable		Clerk		Treasurer	
Assistant/Controller		Controller			
Auditor		Credit and Collection			

ADMINISTRATIVE			
Administrative Assistant		Receptionist	
Clerk/General Office		Switch Board Operator	
Executive Secretary/Secretary		Telecommunications	
Mail Room		Typist	
Office Manager		Word Processor	
HUMAN RESOURCES			
Benefits		Personnel Coordinator	
Compensation		Personnel Manager	
Corporate Travel Planner*		Recruiter	
Meeting Planner*		Safety Specialist/Security	
Personnel Assistant		Training and Development	
Personnel Clerk			
SALES/MARKETING			
Account Executive		Product Manager	
Account Representative		Public Relations	
Inside Sales		Research Analyst	
Intangible Sales		Sales Assistant/Administrator	
Marketing Analyst		Sales Manager	
Marketing Coordinator		Sales Representative	
Marketing Manager		Tangible Sales Representative	
Outside Sales		Telemarketing	

*NOTE: Positions may also fall under communications.

DATA PROCESSING			
Analyst		Programmer	
Consultant		Repair Person	
CRT/Data Entry Clerk		Software Technician	
Engineer		Technical Support Personnel	
Hardware Technician		Technician	
Operator		Systems Integrator	
ENGINEERING			
Applications Engineer		Material Engineer	
CAD/CAM		Mechanical Engineer	
Chemical Engineer		Process Engineer	
Civil Engineer		Product Engineer	
Computer Operator (Hardware/Software)		Project Engineer	
Design Engineer		Quality Assurance Engineer	
Draftsperson		Sales Engineer	
Electrical Engineer		Structural Engineer	
Environmental Engineer		Technical Engineer	
Field Service Technician		Technical Writer	
Industrial Engineer			
OPERATIONS/SERVICE			
Buyer		Inventory Control Supervisor	
Client Service		Operations Manager	
Customer Service Representative		Purchasing Manager	
Expediter		Quality Control/Assurance Coordinator	
Import/Export Clerk			

CONSTRUCTION			
Estimator		Project Manager	
General Contractor		Sub Contractor	
Landscape		Superintendent	
HEALTHCARE/MEDICAL			
Administrator		Records	
Dental		Research	
Doctor		Social Worker	
Nurse		Technician	
Nutritionist		Technologist	
Patient Services		Therapist	
Pharmacist			
LAW			
Corporate Law		Legal Secretary	
Lawyer		Paralegal	
INSURANCE			
Actuary		Life/Health	
Agent		Property/Casualty	
Broker		Risk Manager	
Claims Adjuster		Sales	
Claims Examiner		Underwriter	
BANKING			
Closing Officer		Loan Processor/Officer	
Head Teller		Mortgage	
Investments		Teller	
LABORATORY			
Chemical/Biology		Laboratory Supervisor	
Chemist		Laboratory Technician	
Electronic Engineer		Research & Development	

NOTE: These positions are broken down by industry as they are often found only in that particular field.

RETAIL			
Branch Manager		Store Manager	
General Manager		Window Dresser	
Sales Clerk			
ART/ADVERTISING			
Art Supervisor		Graphics	
Artist		Layout/Paste Up	
Design			
REAL ESTATE			
Agent		Closing Processor	
Broker		Property Manager	

TYPES OF EMPLOYERS

Next, place a ✓ mark next to the industries you have experience in or those you have an interest in and want to research.

Advertising		Insurance	
Aircraft (Airline Industry)		Law	
Automotive		Law Enforcement	
Banking		Manufacturing	
Brokerage		Medical	
Chemical		Non-Profit	
Computer		Oil and Gas	
Construction		Paper and Packaging	
Consulting		Personnel	
Cosmetic		Pharmaceutical	
Data Processing		Photography	
Direct Mail		Printing	
Education		Public Relations	
Electrical		Publishing	
Electronics		Publications	
Environmental		Retail	
Financial		Real Estate	
Floral		Security	
Foods (Science, Beverage, Service, Preparation)		Service	
Government		Sports	
Healthcare		Telecommunications	
Hospitality		Transportation/Travel	
Import/Export		Utilities	
Industrial		Waste Management	

NOTE: The above list is a general guide to most major industries. You will find many advertisements listed under these headings in your local newspapers.

Now that you have determined your qualifications and interests, do some research on the industry and career you have selected. **A good starting place is your local library**. Most libraries have a business section and the librarian will lead you in the right direction. Check for the ***"Dictionary of Occupational Titles"***, which is an informative reference guide that defines each job position in detail. Next, find the names of leaders in the industries you have chosen and place a telephone call to them. (An absolute goldmine of contacts and valuable sources are available in ***"Professional's Job Finder"*** by **Daniel Lauber**).

Your conversation should go something like:

"Hello _____ I understand you are a leader in _____ . My name is _____ and I need your advice, do you have just a moment? I am interested in getting a position in your field and hope to achieve some of the success you have earned. How did you get started? Why do you enjoy your position? Would you encourage me to pursue a career in _____?" If yes, "why?" If no, "why not?" "Do you have any advice on how to break into _____ or to upgrade my experience in _____?" "Who do you know that could utilize someone with my credentials?"

This conversation is your time to **sell yourself** -- so tell them why someone should hire you. (They may be so impressed with your background and personality that they will want to interview you or know someone who would.)

End the conversation with, "Thank you for all your help and I wish you continued success."

Be sure to **write a thank you note to this individual** for his/her time and courtesy. The contacts you make through these efforts can be invaluable to your career.

NOTE: If you are on the shy side and have a hard time calling someone, a professional business letter requesting the same information is also appropriate.

You may decide, after talking with enough people in your chosen industry, to forego this particular career. On the other hand, your efforts may convince you that you have made a good choice.

ONCE YOU DETERMINE A FIRM DIRECTION of the type of position you want to pursue and have research to back up your decision, it is time to put together a resume.

Before you move on to Chapter 3 complete the following checklist.

CHECKLIST FOR PREPARING TO INTERVIEW SUCCESSFULLY

	HAVE YOU:	**YES**	**NO**
1.)	Identified your likes and dislikes/strengths and weaknesses?	_____	_____
2.)	Outlined your talents and achievements?	_____	_____
3.)	Determined specific job positions to pursue?	_____	_____
4.)	Selected industries to research thoroughly?	_____	_____
5.)	Researched occupations/industries related to your career goals?	_____	_____
6.)	Interviewed individuals by writing or calling?	_____	_____

At this point you should complete all 6 steps before writing your resume. If you missed one and are tempted to jump ahead anyway, remember that employers don't always hire the most experienced candidate, **just the best prepared.** Jumping ahead before completing your job search plan is like putting up the walls of a house before the foundation is complete. It might hold up temporarily, however, six months down the road, you'll end up with a house full of cracks. **Isn't something as important as your job search worth the time and effort?** After all, we spend more time at work than at home. Can you afford not to be prepared for something that will affect your entire life and happiness? **OKAY IT'S TIME TO HAVE SOME FUN!** Let's go create a cover letter and resume that will get you great interviews.

chapter three

How to write a GREAT cover Letter & RESUME

HOW TO WRITE A GREAT COVER LETTER AND RESUME

Cover letters are as important as resumes! To be most effective, cover letters need to be individually typed rather than printed like your resume. Each letter should be geared specifically to the position for which you are applying. <u>There is nothing more unprofessional than submitting a sloppy cover-letter or even none at all.</u> Remember, it is only necessary to include your salary history (see page 38) when specifically requested in the advertisement. Otherwise, **do not include your past income or references.** In this case, "less is more."

Following are <u>two examples of cover letters that are not only recommended</u>, but have been personally and successfully used. These letters may generally be used when responding to a newspaper advertisement.

TIP: If you are planning on sending an unsolicited resume or have heard of an opening through networking, you can still use these letters. Simply substitute, "in response to your recent advertisement," with an explanation of how you heard about the company.

NOTE: Make sure your cover letter is on matching or coordinating paper with your resume.

Date

Company Name
Address
City, State, Zip Code
Attention: Hiring Official (Use specific name if available)

Dear Hiring Official,

"NOTHING VENTURED; NOTHING GAINED"

Undertaking chances is the one element of success for which we maintain complete control. I am venturing on new career opportunities for the New Year and was impressed with your recent advertisement in (name of the newspaper). After researching your companys history and discovering what a progressive firm you are, I am confident that a meeting between us would benefit us both.

'Allow me to introduce myself, I am a (job title) in the (industry). I am a highly motivated, successful administrator with an excellent eye for hiring and training sales and office support staff. I have a proven track record developing sales individuals to recognize and fulfill their potential. Even though I am thorough and detail oriented, I am able to see the "whole picture" and complete long term goals.

My superior client relations skills, built through telephone conversations and personal business visits, enabled me to maintain several key accounts during my career changes. In addition to my strong management and sales abilities, I am extremely innovative and have developed new and creative ideas now implemented in the (name of) industry.

I maintain flexibility in career fields and am capable of effectively demonstrating my proven skills, experience and personality in an interview.

Looking forward to hearing from you and learning more about (name of the company).

Respectfully,

(Your Name)

Enclosure

NOTE: It is important that you incorporate your own skills and abilities in this letter. Be sure to use adjectives and action words that reflect your uniqueness. (See page 30)

If this first cover letter is too assertive for your own style, the next one is just as

compelling, yet more conservative.

Sample Letter Two

Date

Company Name
Address
City, State Zip Code
Attention: Hiring Official

Dear Hiring Official:

Your recent advertisement in the (name of newspaper) was most impressive and certainly got my attention. Outlined for your convenience, please find a summary of my experience .

(Your Name Centered and Bold)

SUMMARY OF QUALIFICATIONS

PERSONNEL Highly motivated and <u>successful administrator</u> with an excellent eye for hiring and training sales and office support staff.

MANAGEMENT <u>Proven track record</u> developing sales individuals to recognize and fulfill their potential. Superb delegator and authority on time management. Thorough and detail oriented, yet able to see the "whole picture" and complete long term goals.

INNOVATIVE Have <u>developed new</u> and creative <u>ideas currently utilized</u> in the (name of industry).

CLIENT RELATIONS <u>Superior rapport</u> built <u>with customers</u> through telephone conversations and personal business visits. <u>Expanded</u> and maintained <u>several key clients</u> throughout my career changes.

EDUCATION In addition to my college background, I firmly believe in being the best one can be. Actively involved in _____ (list any seminars, special training or volunteer organizations).

PERSONAL QUALITIES <u>Positive</u> and <u>upbeat attitude</u> enables me to look at the glass as *half full* rather than half empty. <u>Integrity</u> both in business and personal life has provided me a good reputation and pride in my professionalism.

Enclosed find my resume for your consideration. I look forward to meeting you and personally demonstrating my skills and experience in an interview.

Sincerely,
Your Name
Enclosure   **NOTE:**   **This cover letter is ideal for individuals without a great deal of work experience. It summarizes your abilities and qualities rather than focusing on your job history.**

THE WORD "RESUME" MEANS *SUMMARY*

A resume should be a professional reflection of your job history and <u>personal style.</u> Keep in mind you may need to compose more than one resume or summary of qualifications for different positions. You will also need to include a clever cover letter. This technique is especially important if you are sending resumes to companies, rather than applying in person.

Have your resume professionally typeset and printed. (This can be done on a desktop publisher , a word processor or at a print-shop). Start out with at least 25 copies (you can always get more) and 25 blank sheets of matching paper for your cover letters and salary history. Do not forget the letter size envelopes!* **These added touches will be noticed and the cost of your resume and job search expenses are tax deductible!**

Word of caution! **PROOFREAD...PROOFREAD...PROOFREAD.** Most printers will not take responsibility for mistakes once your resume is printed. <u>Have at least two people (besides yourself) carefully edit your resume</u>, as it is very easy to overlook an error. If an error is not caught and the printing is completed, you will be responsible for all the costs in printing. **A mistake at this stage of your job search could cost you an interview and possibly a job offer.**

Choose either ivory or gray paper for your resume and cover letter. **<u>You want your resume to stand out from all the rest of the resumes companies receive.</u>**

*****NOTE:** 8¹⁄₂ x 11" matching envelopes are also quite impressive and your resume will not arrive folded.

Details like correct spelling and grammar, matching paper and professional printing all add up to reflect that you care about your image and are a cut above the average person. In this day and age, with positions at a premium, **you need to go the extra mile to even get the chance to be considered.**

TIP: Do not use bright or "off the wall" paper to get the employer's attention. It is inappropriate and unprofessional.

Added Touch: Type the employer's address on the envelope rather than handwriting it.

In most cases, a one page resume is preferred. However, for those of you with more than 10 years of experience, you may need an additional page.

Do not be wordy or embellish the truth too much. You may receive a position over your head and then be back where you started from -- looking for a new job. Employers do check references from your past experience or schooling. Honesty is the best policy in writing a good resume.

Remember, <u>resumes do not get people jobs</u> -- **people do**. Resumes should have just enough interesting and exciting tidbits to get you in the door -- **the rest is up to you.**

When composing a resume that gets results, you need to be in a results oriented state of mind. Use action words to describe yourself. Action words will reflect your positive attitude and high energy level and promote the company's interest enough to invite you in for an interview.

To get you started on writing or updating your resume, following are some great action words to include in your description.

Actively Involved	Delegate	Implement	Prepare
Administrative	Design	Increase	Proactive
Attained	Develop	Initiate	Produce
Authority	Devised	Integral	Promote
Contribute	Energetic	Manage	Recognize
Coordinate	Enhanced	Maximize	Resolve
Complete	Establish	Motivate	Revise
Compose	Execute	Negotiate	Selective
Create	Facilitate	Orchestrate	Streamline
Creative	Fulfill	Organize	Teach
Dedicated	Generate	Originate	Troubleshoot

You can also refer to the list of qualities companies look for on **page 12 in Chapter Two** for additional words to enhance your resume and to avoid duplicating yourself. It is important to avoid overusing the same word. **Do not use the same word MORE THAN TWO TIMES on your resume.**

TIP: Always start with your most recent position. Include dates and months of employment for each company. If you eliminate dates, it sends up a red flag to many employers. If you are not currently employed and have not updated your resume to reflect that you have already left your company, update it immediately. An employer once passed up interviewing a candidate because the most recent position on his resume stated "to present" even though he had left one month earlier. The employer needed someone to start immediately and thought this person would need to give notice. **Moral:** Honesty, Honesty, Honesty!

When considering your resume, start with a rough draft. **You will be making a great deal of changes.** Go back to the start of your career and list all the jobs you have held. Write a detailed description of each position, including all of your achievements and promotions (these descriptions will be narrowed down in the process).

If you have been in the marketplace more than 20 years, concentrate on the last 10 to 15 years of your experience. You can always fill in the rest during the course of an interview.

After you have walked down memory lane and compiled all the facts, now it is time to **incorporate action words** to describe each responsibility to reflect **results!**

Example:

A.   "Answered customer questions and handled complaints."   (Task Oriented)

B.   **"Resolved client problems to ensure customer satisfaction."**   **(Results Oriented)**

NOTICE THE DIFFERENCE A CHOICE OF WORDS CAN MAKE ?

> **TIP:**   Only include part-time jobs if you have not yet had a full-time position or if the part-time experience relates to the position you are applying for.

Next, it is time to edit your rough draft and pare it down to what you should include in your final resume. **Eliminate** any duplications or **redundancies** (save all the extra tidbits to review in the actual interview). It is important to include specifics, such as, model of computer/type of software/name of sales training received, etc.

If the details are fuzzy on some of the projects or specific types of equipment you have worked on, call an old friend, co-worker or boss who you've have worked with and see if they can help you remember. It is worth the call and they may even help you recall something you have totally forgotten.

Your resume should be a written advertisement selling you! If you are still having trouble "putting it all together", it may be time to hire a professional resume service to help smooth out the rough edges. Work closely with your contact to ensure they have all the information necessary to accurately capture your personality on paper. Ask to see several samples of their work before you hire a resume service and do not hesitate to request references from their past clients.

Prices range from $50 to $500 for most resume services. A higher price does not guarantee better quality. **Be sure to ask if the price quoted includes printing costs!** Find out how much is charged for extra copies as needed. Most reputable resume services will keep you in their database for future updates. Inquire if they automatically delete your file after a certain amount of time or if you have a lifetime place in their computer file. This point can be important for future career updates without having to start from scratch. (Most resume companies should provide you with your disk).

A terrific resume of which you are proud will not only get you in the door, it will be a wonderful tool in giving you the extra self confidence you need to make a great impression. **Remember, you are not only investing in yourself, but also in the rest of your career!** By taking the extra time and effort, you will be excited and pleased with the results!

GUIDELINES TO WRITING A PROFESSIONAL RESUME

THAT GETS INTERVIEWS!

---

1.   Be descriptive yet brief. Use a layout that is easy to read and doesn't appear crowded.

2.   **Objectives are not necessary** - have you ever seen an objective where the individual wants a boring unchallenging position? Your cover letter should outline what you are looking for. **EMPLOYERS USE OBJECTIVES TO SCREEN YOU OUT-NOT IN!**

3.   Write in <u>present tense</u> for your current position and <u>past tense</u> for previous ones.

4.   **One page resumes are most enticing.** <u>Statistics show a typical employer</u> will <u>read your resume about 30 seconds</u> before deciding on whether to bring you in for an interview.

5.   Only use bullet points for highlights, not on each job duty. (Keep it to 6 bullets per page)

6.   Always <u>start</u> with your most recent position first.

7.   Use **action words** to describe your responsibilities..

8.   <u>Remember a resume is a written advertisement selling you!</u> Imagine a television or magazine ad that caught your attention. Good ads **sell benefits** and image. **What is your resume projecting?**

9.   If you have your resume professionally printed or printed from a laser printer- **DO NOT USE RECYCLABLE PAPER-**it flakes off the page when folded and the employer will receive a resume with patches of ink or words missing.

     NOTE: When an employer reads your resume he should be able to visualize what kind of employee you are.   The employers needs to be motivated to pick up the phone and call you for an interview.   Be objective when viewing your resume. **When you look at your resume does it really describe you and your personality?** Are you proud to hand it out? If not--go back and re-edit your resume when you are in a positive frame of mind.

The following are two resume formats that have been well received by employers and can be easily typed on a word processor.

Name
Address
City, State Zip Code   **Phone Number**

Education_____

Bachelor of Science - Industrial/Organizational Psychology
University of Illinois - Champaign/Urbana

Professional History_____

NAME OF COMPANY   *07/91 to Present*
Project Manager

Coordination of client recruitment research projects including database searches,
candidate sourcing and development of assignment specifications. Responsible for
generating repeat sales from major clients and **initiating** client follow up as needed.
Major clients include: (Name major clients.)

NAME OF COMPANY   *07/89 to 05/91*
Billing Inquiry Representative

Responsible for customer service, **resolution** of billing problems, recommending service
to customers and **negotiating** billing claims to **increase** customer satisfaction.
Additionally accountable for training employees, data base management and computer
operations.

> Chaired sales committee which **implemented** and increased new
> revenue streams.
> **Created** several new forms to **improve** in-house services operation.
> Worked in management capacity for immediate supervisor.
> <u>**Duties Included:**</u>
> **Effectively** supervising staff comprised of twenty peers.
> Managing and **delegating** staff workload.
> Coordinating several projects **simultaneously.**

VOLUNTEER SERVICES_____

Speakers Bureau / Chairperson 1989 - Present
Fund Raising Committee / YWCA 1991 - 1992
Training Facilitator / Make A Wish Foundation 1990

ADDITIONAL TRAINING / SKILLS

Computer literate IBM PC - Lotus 1.2.3. , Word Perfect 5.1., Quarkpress
TOTAL QUALITY MANAGEMENT SEMINAR 1992
Earned certification in **Advanced Sales Leadership** - Northwestern University 1991

NAME

Address
City, State Zip Code
Phone Number

ACHIEVEMENTS/AWARDS

Midwest Account Executive of year 1980 (Rookie Year)
Ranked in top five in nation 1980 - 1985 (125 offices)
Nominated Producing Manager of Year 1981
Inducted to the Hall of Fame 1985
Authored book *GETTING HIRED IN THE '90s* 1991

PROFESSIONAL EXPERIENCE

9/89 to Present

Company Name
Account Manager/Independent Contractor
Market employment services via telephone and client visits
Effectively manage personnel functions for 50 clients
Orchestrate hiring, training and evaluation of new employees
Recruit, interview and consult candidates regarding career moves

Highlights
    Increased office production and client base by 45 percent
    Team leader for program to create and implement client
    presentation and training materials generating $50,000 in orders

---

7/87 to 9/89

Company Name
6/88 to 9/89
General Manager
Developed and executed corporate identity program for start-up operation
including: name, logo, marketing materials, training program and advertising
strategies
Complete autonomy for new division
Selected, hired, successfully trained and motivated staff of 12
Created innovative and top revenue producing On-Premise Division

Highlights
    Regional top 20: first, fourth, fifth and sixth months
    Grossed $300,000 first year

7/87 to 6/88

Sales Manager
Successfully managed staff of six account executives
Generated $100,000 in placement revenue

Tip: It is not necessary to print "resume on the top of the page.

NAME

10/85 - 7/87

Company Name
Account Executive
Basic responsibilities of "Account Manager" position

10/79 - 10/85

Company Name
Account Executive/Sales Manager
Promoted after 18 months to manager

Highlights

Earned number two position in nation. Rookie year
(five hundred employees)
Only Account Executive in nation to work four days
per week and produce number one status in 1985

EDUCATIONAL BACKGROUND

Name of University
Courses Studied or Major
Specialized Training
Real Estate 101
Tom Hopkins Sales Training
Zig Ziglar Seminar
Dale Carnegie
Computer Literate / IBM PC-Word Perfect 5.0, 5.1

NOTE: Always put your educational background first if you have a degree. If you have not received a degree, list any schooling or additional training other than high school at the bottom.

TIP: Do not list personal information, such as, marital status, age, etc. It is not necessary to include your reasons for leaving companies. It is recommended that you include your months of employment as well as years. Otherwise, employers may think you are trying to cover large gaps in employment history.

Now that your resume is ready to go, you need some direction as to where to send them. **Remember, mass mailings can be very expensive and ineffective.** Chapter Four will provide you with information on how to direct your energies toward results!

TIP: Carry your original resumes in a professional folder to ensure that the resume and recommendation letters do not get wrinkled or torn. If you have several examples of your work or testimonial letters, be sure to enclose the originals in plastic sheet covers to keep them fresh looking. **Always have several extra xerox copies of letters in your folder or briefcase to give to the employer to keep rather than expecting them to read the letters on the spot or make their own copies!** If you have not accumulated enough experience to get a reference letter from an employer, get one from a college teacher or a professional, highlighting your placability.

When an advertisement or a company requests a salary history, what they are looking for is a **one page summary** of the positions you have held, length of employment and your starting and ending salaries. Include any raises, promotions, bonuses or commissions. This information should be **typed on a separate page from your resume and cover letter** on matching paper. **DO NOT include your salary history with your resume** unless the company specifically requests it.

Following is an example of a salary history.

SALARY HISTORY

Name of Company	Title	Length of Employment	Starting Salary	Ending Salary
XYZ Company	Office Manager	1989 - Present	$34,500	$43,900
XYZ Company	Administrative Assistant	1987 - 1989 (Promoted)	$28,000	$31,500
ABC Company	Sales Coordinator	1984 - 1987	$25,000	$27,000 + bonus

---

NOTE: Start with your most recent position first. List your last four or five positions only. If you have held more than five positions in the past 15 years, do not include the remaining number of positions.

chapter
four

Where to START LOOKING for a new POSITION

WHERE TO START LOOKING FOR A NEW POSITION

NETWORKING

As discussed in Chapter Two, business contacts are extremely important in uncovering hidden career opportunities. **Tell everyone you know and meet that you are active in the job market**. When individuals are unemployed, they have a tendency to hide from the business world. Encourage yourself to stay active and communicate with past business contacts and friends. **The ideal position will not come knocking on your door -- you need to go out and find it.**

Start networking by making a list of everyone you know:

Business Acquaintances and Business Associates (Be discreet)
Church or Synagogue Members
Clients*
College Placement Offices (Even schools you have not attended)
Doctors and Lawyers
Ex-Bosses and Past Co-workers
Friends and Health Club Members
Job Fairs
Support Groups and Associations
Local Unemployment Offices
Seminars (on related industries)
On-line Networks i.e. Prodigy/Internet / Kinexus (See Page 49)
Free-Lance or temporary assignments

After you have compiled your list with telephone numbers, start at the top and call these individuals to inform them of your intentions. **Be upfront, ask them if they know of anything available for someone in your field**. They may be willing to make some calls for you or keep their eyes open.

*NOTE: I do not advocate telling clients, however, if you have an unusually close relationship, they may be a good source of contacts.

ADVERTISEMENTS

Depending on where you live, ads can be a viable employment source. However, this method can be extremely time consuming and some ads can be very misleading.

Many top corporations do not advertise because their name alone is a calling card and they do not have the staff to screen all the resumes or calls they receive. Also, the larger firms usually promote from within for the higher level positions, leaving mostly entry level positions open.

On the other end of the spectrum, many small to medium size firms will not advertise because they have a hard time competing with the "top" companies and drawing the right people to a relatively unknown of name in the industry.

Remember, advertisements are written to get you to call. Read between the lines! Many are misrepresented to get you in the door and sound much more exciting than they actually are.

Once you have decided to scan the want ads, be prepared to start at the beginning and read each ad carefully. The **job categories are not always clear cut** and the ideal opportunity may be placed under a heading of which you would never imagine. The larger the city in which you live, the more ads through which you will need to look.

Circle each ad that applies to you, even those of which you are not sure you meet their requirements. Remember, companies are advertising for that perfect person. Many employers are willing to compromise a bit. So, if the ad reads: college degree a must or desired, and you only have two years of college - **GO FOR IT!** On the other hand, if they ask for several years technical experience and you are just starting out, do not waste your time and energy.

Below is a simple worksheet that will help organize your job search and assist you with your follow up routine.

Date Called	Company Name	Contact	Position Applied For	Date Resume Sent	Interview Date	Date To Follow Up	Comments

TIP: Make several copies of this form and keep them in a three ring binder for an easy and organized follow up.

Most companies run their ads in the Sunday edition, however, read the daily newspaper to check for those that may have opened up mid-week.

It is best to **call first thing Monday morning** so you can be assured an interview time.* (Use Monday afternoon for your resume mailings and any research on the companies you plan on interviewing with during the week.) If you are currently employed, plan on taking off two to three personal or vacation days to call the ads and schedule interviews. It is not always a wise idea to call from your desk at work because someone may overhear you or you may be interrupted. Do not wait until lunch to call or the hiring official may also be away at lunch. If the screening representative is not available, it is best to call back rather than leave a message. Most hiring authorities will be too busy to call you back and you may miss out on a good opportunity.

Only schedule two to three interviews per day. Otherwise the positions will start to blend together and you will not appear fresh and enthusiastic. You need to have a clear head to present yourself well and make a good decision.

Allow yourself plenty of time between interviews to insure promptness. The ideal time to interview is between 9:00 a.m. and 11:00 a.m. The employer is still alert and has not yet had to face too many problems of the day. Another good time is right after the lunch hour, when the employers may be more relaxed. Late interviews after normal business hours will often find you meeting with a frazzled, tired interviewer who wants nothing more than to go home.

*TIP: This also shows your enthusiasm if you are "up and at 'em" early on Monday morning. The employer gets the idea you are anxious to work.

Another reason to interview during business hours, is so you can see how the employees interact with each other. You can view first hand the pace of the office and the overall morale of the company.

In larger employment markets, many ads are placed by employment agencies. When an advertisement states "Call our Rep" or "Client company is looking for...," the ad was placed by an agency. Some agencies use bait and switch ads to attract your attention. Once you are in their office, they say the position is filled or you are not qualified. Some may try to convince you to go on a different opportunity they currently have available.

In defense of the more reputable agencies or search firms, many are a viable source of unadvertised positions. You need to ask around and locate a referral of an agency in your area who can best benefit you.

TIP: Many ads are blind ads (ads that only list the telephone number and no company name). Call your local reverse directory and supply them with the phone number and they will tell you the name of the company and its address. This way you can investigate the company before you even call. **Be careful if you are currently employed when sending resumes to blind P.O. Boxes.** It may be your present company! Check your local newspaper to see if they offer services to screen your resume from those companies you do not want it forwarded to. You are taking a big risk if you are currently employed and sending resumes to blind P.O. Boxes.

Now that you have selected the ads to which you want to respond, **fill out the worksheet on page 42 and practice your telephone demeanor.*** Be upbeat, positive and confident.

*NOTE: Many employers are turned off by monotone telephone voices. It is imperative to sound enthusiastic and energetic in order to convince them to interview you.

Your conversation could go something like this:

"Hello (hiring official's name), how are you today? My name is _____. Your ad for _____

position sure caught my attention! Did you write the ad? (Chances are they did, especially if they work

in personnel.) It is very good. I am interested in hearing more about _____ position. Would you

please describe it in more detail?"

Be prepared for hiring officials to screen you out by asking questions about your

background before you are told about the position. Your main objective is to have the

opportunity to show them your credentials. If they ask you to send in a resume, tell them you

plan to be in their area later that day and can drop it off in person. (Hopefully when you get

there, you can at least shake their hand or spend a few minutes talking with them.) At the very

least, your resume will not end up on the bottom of the pile and they can match a face with the

name. **Employers will appreciate your extra effort.**

If salary is not listed in the ad, **DO NOT** ask about it. The company may or may not

volunteer this information. Some employers will request what salary range you are looking for

or are currently earning. Do not commit to a figure at this point. Instead, tell them something

along these lines: **"I am currently negotiable and am open to a fair offer. The most**

important priority to me right now is to affiliate myself with a good company such as

yours."

Remember, if you talk money at this stage, you could end up talking yourself right out the door. Although you are taking a chance going to the interview not knowing the salary, the only thing you might lose in the process is an hour of your time. **That is why you need to develop a screening process of your own so you are not running all over town on every interview you accept.** Many employers will bring in everyone who answers the ad. Others get so many responses that they are very selective. Thoughtful questions like "How long has this position been available?" or "Could you tell me a little about the company's philosophy?" will help you decide if you want to invest your time into the interview. You can initially make the appointment while on the telephone, think about it and later call to cancel the appointment if you change your mind.

TIP: Some employers will quote the lowest salary figure in their range. (To screen you out or hire the best employee for the least possible amount of money.) The employer may have flexibility of several thousand dollars in his range or budget for the "perfect" person. **Wait to negotiate your salary until the company has had a chance to interview you and decides it wants to hire you.** At this point, you will be surprised how flexible the company can be if you are a bit above their range. Another point in your favor when not mentioning a figure up front, (even if you want more than the company is quoting) is you may be compared to other individuals who are willing to take less, however, you are more qualified and worth paying the salary you request. How many times have you set a figure of what you can afford or are willing to pay for something you really want and have ended up paying more? Remember that new car you just had to have? Or the great looking outfit you could not live without? Keep in mind employers are human too.

AGENCIES

(Alias Headhunters, Search Firms, Employment Consultants, etc.)

All major metropolitan areas have several different services to choose from. Some agencies specialize, others are generalists. You can find them listed in the yellow pages, but the best way is to be recommended by a previous satisfied client or applicant.

Call for an appointment rather than sending an unsolicited resume. Most headhunters do read unsolicited resumes but do not spend a great deal of time on someone who is sending one to every agency or with whom they have not personally talked to or met. Agencies prefer referrals. If you go through the telephone book, ask for the most experienced counselor/recruiter or manager. **Make a good first impression, as this person can be most influential and beneficial to your career.*** If the recruiter likes you and is impressed, he will decide to represent you. If a recruiter is not excited or impressed by you he can decide not to represent you. You are not paying a fee, therefore, it is the agency's choice to work with you or not. Most search firms or agencies get paid by the company who is hiring.

Consulting firms differ from search firms and agencies. Some consulting firms charge as much as $5,000.00 to write your resume and give you leads. You are responsible for arranging your own interviews and do not have any guarantee on whether or not you find a job. **I DO NOT ENDORSE THESE FIRMS.** I personally recommend only the agencies where the employer pays the fee.

---

*TIP: Remember, this is an interview too! Prepare for this just as you would if it were a normal job interview.

Once you have arranged an interview with a recruiter, follow all the same interviewing tips you will find outlined in Chapter Five. One word of advice, do not insinuate you can do a better job at finding your own position or that you are just looking around. **The recruiter is a trained expert in his or her field a**nd will NOT work with candidates who do not treat them with the respect he or she deserve.

<u>Trust this individual and take his or her advice.</u> If you do not have a good rapport with your counselor you can request to deal with someone else in the firm or go to another agency. Take time to outline exactly what type of career you seek (recruiters are not trained career counselors and do not want to nor have the expertise to advise which career is best for you). Headhunters that do specialize in a particular industry are very knowledgeable about their own industry and can guide you. However, if you are in need of an actual career counselor, it is best to go to an individual who has in-depth knowledge of helping people choose which career may be best for them. <u>If you are making a career change or seeking an entry level position and are not sure for what you are best suited, seek an experienced career counselor first.</u>

When using an agency, be cooperative and flexible (the search firm may have an idea for an opportunity you may not have previously considered). You need to be firm about your desires and do not let an overly enthusiastic recruiter talk you into anything you do not want. **Keep an open mind and be honest.**

Dealing with a search firm can be the most efficient and discreet way of locating a good opportunity.

BENEFITS OF USING A SEARCH FIRM

✓ Saves time on interviewing with companies that will not pay what you are worth or in which you would have no interest.

✓ Provides access to unadvertised openings. (Hidden Job Market)

✓ Negotiates salary - usually resulting in a higher figure than you could get for yourself (remember, the higher the salary you get, the more money your recruiter makes -- he is on your side).

✓ Provides up-front knowledge of the company, before your interview.

✓ Offers better odds than going through advertisements (less competition). Good headhunters will typically send their top three to five candidates. With newspaper ads, you may be up against 50 to 250 applicants.

✓ Represents quality companies who are willing to pay a fee to attract top talent and views their employees as assets worth paying for.

BENEFITS OF ENROLLING IN A CANDIDATE DATABASE

Computers are becoming more and more instrumental in facilitating successful recruitment efforts. Since many top corporations realize how cost effective and productive database recruitment is, if you ignore this growing trend you may be left out in the cold. Kinexus is the nations largest candidate database. For a nominal fee they will include you in their database which is distributed to Fortune 1000 companies, medium-sized brand manufacturers, smaller high-tech companies and financial firms, just to name a few. This instant access to employers who may not otherwise place an ad or use an agency, is another smart networking opportunity for you to take advantage of. (**See page 108 for more information and application form**) .

✓ Low, one time cost to advertise yourself to hundreds of prospective employers.

✓ Savings to you in terms of cost of paper, postage and time of actually sending out your resumes to companies.

✓ Access to companies who may only utilize their computer data base to recruit for a particular position.

✓ Get an edge on your competition--you will have your resume right in front of the employer before anyone who is replying to an ad would.

✓ Many personnel recruiters prefer looking at a computer to screen resumes rather than go through page after page of cover letter and resumes.

chapter five

You've got the Interview... NOW WHAT?

Okay, so you have lined up the interview. What do you wear? At one time, the only appropriate interview outfit was a navy blue suit and a white shirt or blouse. That attire is still acceptable, however, if you look washed out in navy or do not feel like a million dollars in that suit, other options are available.

A conservative business suit is recommended, yet you can also be somewhat creative. Like the resume, let the outfit you wear reflect your personal style and personality. **If you do not currently own a business suit, it is an investment in your future you cannot afford to ignore.** Make sure when you make your selection of clothing that you have a proper fit, no tears, wrinkles or missing buttons. If you are currently working in a casual environment where dressing up for an outside interview would look suspicious, go home first to change!

Do not wait until the last minute to select an outfit. Remember, you will not get a second chance to make a good first impression. **The employer will judge your overall appearance within the first few seconds upon meeting you.**

Interview clothing and accessories:

WOMEN	
DOs	**DON'Ts**
Conservative business dress or suit	Extremely bright colors or wild patterns
Lightly applied makeup	Perfume (heavy) or excessive make-up
Wear a watch	Patterned/colored stockings (no runs in stockings)
Medium to low heels (1" - 2", polished)	3" high heels or boots
Long hair put up/pulled back	Evening apparel or pant suits
Small amount of jewelry (small earrings, one ring)	Large pieces of jewelry (bracelets, ankle bracelets, etc.)
Clear nail polish (short to medium length nails)	Bright nail polish
Small purse/briefcase	Smoking (even if they offer) or coffee
Fresh breath	Chewing gum or mints during the interview

MEN	
DOs	**DON'Ts**
Tailored business suit (matching suit coat and pants)	Unmatched jacket and pants
Clean and pressed white/ivory shirt	Smoking (even if they offer) or coffee
Conservative tie	Cologne (heavy)
Clean shaven face/mustache trimmed	5 o'clock shadow
Watch	Double breasted suit coat
Shined shoes	Boots or casual shoes
Over-the-calf dark socks	Hat
Manicured Hands	Dirt under fingernails
Fresh breath	Chewing gum or mints during the interview

If you live in a cold climate and must wear boots, bring your shoes and slip them on outside the office before you enter. In warmer climates it is **not acceptable to wear sleeveless** or three-quarter-length sleeves -- your arms must be covered to the wrist, ladies, keep your skirts close to or just below the knee. Even in the summer, pantyhose are a must, and **never wear sandals.**

What you need to project with your image is confidence. **You always want to dress as though you are already successful, even when you are just starting out.** Remember to have back up outfits when second or third interviews are required. The hiring authority believes that during the interview, you will be at your 100% best. Some offices have a casual dress code and if you dress better than the employer does, they may feel you would not fit in or are too qualified for the position. That is why if you dress conservatively, yet professionally (middle of the road), you will fit in almost anywhere. **The most important thing to keep in mind while making your selection of what to wear is that you want them to remember you, not what you wore that day!**

The night before the interview is important in the interview process. Studies show that you will feel more refreshed with your normal night's sleep. If you usually go to bed at 10:00 p.m., do not go to sleep at 8:00 p.m. to get extra sleep. The extra sleep may disrupt your regular routine. Lay out your clothes the evening before so you are not rushed and can spend a few extra minutes getting ready. Allow yourself plenty of time; the more hurried you feel, the more likely you are to feel frazzled!

If possible, take a trial run out to the company the day before to familiarize yourself with the route and the area. This way, you can judge the time allotment for the commute. Being late is a sure way of loosing points with the employer. I suggest **allowing yourself an extra half-hour of driving time**. Even when you arrive 30 minutes early, you can use that time to relax and practice some of your interviewing answers. If you do arrive 30 minutes ahead of time, sit in your car and wait 15 minutes before you go into the company. Arriving too early can upset the interviewer's schedule and he or she may feel pressured. Always arrive at least five minutes early. This shows your promptness and enthusiasm.

HOMEWORK

Before the interview, spend some time in the library researching any potential employer for which you plan on working. **This is your livelihood in question. Why leave it to chance?** Just because a company has four walls and a ceiling does not make it financially solid or a good place to work. Ask your local librarian to help you select some reference books that relate to the industry or company to which you are applying. **This information will be invaluable during the interview.** You will be able to ask informed questions and show the employer you have intelligence, initiative and that you took the time to do your homework.

Following is a list of pertinent information to look for in a potential employer:

Competitors

Industry Growth Rate

Location of Headquarters and Satellite Offices

Names and Background Information on Key Company Officials

Product or Service Information

Publicly or Privately Held

Size of the Company

Percentage of the Market

Additional publications you can use in your research include: the business section of your local newspaper, industry trade magazines and local or national business newspapers or magazines. **(i.e. Crains Chicago is an excellent choice for Chicago area readers).** Do not forget asking your friends or business acquaintances if they know anything about the firm to which you are applying. They can be a source of valuable information.

Once you have done your homework, you can now tailor-make several well-informed questions to ask the potential employer. **(Chapter Six will outline which questions can give you the important information you desire.)**

Nothing can help you get hired if you just try and wing it or go into the interview unprepared. **PRACTICE PRACTICE PRACTICE**! Get together with a friend or business associate and conduct a mock interview. Tape yourself and you will hear how your voice sounds. All of your "umms" and "uhs" and "you knows" will come through loud and clear. Everyone hears themselves differently than others do, so be objective and ask your mock

interviewer to give you constructive criticism. Do not take the criticism personally. **We are not taught to interview, we are just expected to know how. Interviewing is a learned skill, not an inherent quality.** After taping yourself (preferably video), watch or listen to yourself and critique what you need to improve on. Practice in the mirror and watch your facial expressions. Listen to the tone of your voice and pay attention to your body language. This activity seems time consuming, however, **would you rather learn at the expense of losing an offer, or beforehand, in the comfort of your home?** You will reach a point where most of your answers are automatic, yet come off as unrehearsed.

After all your preparation and practice, you will feel confident and excited about the interview. Chapter Six will provide all the questions and information you need to achieve your goal -- **GETTING THE JOB OFFER.**

TIP: If your interview is being conducted in a restaurant or hotel - NEVER accept a cocktail. Thank them for the offer and decline politely!

chapter six

The Interview

&

How to GET
The OFFER

THE INTERVIEW

Walk into the interview with shoulders back and a smile on your face. **Be happy to be there.** Make sure to be friendly to everyone! Start with the receptionist by developing a good rapport. She or he may report back to the hiring official of your mood and demeanor. Receptionists have a great deal more influence than you think!

Some companies will start you off by having you fill out the dreaded application. You may say to yourself, **"Why do I have to fill out an application when I went through all the trouble of preparing a great resume?"** Several reasons exist why an employer wants you to complete the application.

First, an employer wants to check your handwriting or printing. Neat printing is strongly recommended. Do not start by printing, get tired and then handwrite the rest of the application. **Be consistent.** Take your time and make sure your spelling is correct. I have seen applicants misspell the title of the position for which they were applying. If you cannot even spell your title correctly, what is your potential for doing a good job?

Another common mistake people make is writing on the application, "see resume." This reference irritates employers. What if they lose the resume or prefer to look at an application? **(Remember, follow directions!!)**

TIP: Remember to bring several original resumes to the interview. You may get the opportunity to meet several people the same day!

NOTE: Most applications ask your reason for leaving companies. If you have been fired over a personality dispute, write: "will discuss." If you were laid off, write: "reduction in staff." If you left for more money, write: "better opportunity." Do not go into detail, leave that for the interview. Employers are leery if you have only left positions for more money. Be sure to include other motivating factors, such as, professional environment or more challenging responsibilities.

While waiting for the hiring official to greet you, take time to observe the office surroundings to give you a feel for the company. Is there complete silence in the office? Do the employees interact well? Are they smiling and enjoying their work?

When the employer greets you, make sure he extends his hand first. Some employers do not like to shake hands. Keep your right hand near your side ready to firmly shake his hand. A nice firm handshake is important. It shows you have confidence. **Women: wimpy, light handshakes are things of the past! Men: do not give the bonecrusher handshake to show your manliness.** Practice on a friend first.

Your initial conversation could sound something like this:

"Hi (hiring official's name), I am (your name). It is a pleasure to meet you." **Smile...smile...smile...and maintain good eye contact.**

When asked to be seated, do not move the chair. Many applicants make the mistake of moving the chair too close to the employer's desk. Do not crowd the employer's space. He wants the chair in a particular place. Once you are seated, make sure to sit upright toward the edge of your seat. **Do not get too comfortable.** Make an opening statement such as, "What a nice office you have." (Some flattering small talk to put them at ease.) Remember, employers can be very nervous, too. If the office is cluttered and strewn with papers, take another avenue,

such as: "Your directions were perfect," or "I am excited to finally meet you, you were so friendly on the telephone." Then, offer your resume and **keep silent**. Give the employer a chance to review your application and resume. Being overly chatty will appear as nervousness. **Keep your eyes on the employer at all times and sit still.** Your hands should be folded in your lap or at your side during the entire interview. It can be too distracting if you use your hands too much during the conversation.

> **TIP:** Many employers feel candidates appear too uptight or nervous during an interview. Do not leave your sense of humor at home. Ninety percent of the hiring decision will be based on personality and how well the company likes you. BE YOURSELF and let the employer see the real you!

Most interviewers will start off the conversation by saying, "Tell me about yourself." This question can be handled in two ways and your response depends on how much you know about the position for which you are applying. Remember, employers are not looking for your life history. **He is interested in learning why he should hire you.** Assuming you are familiar with what the company is looking to hire, your answer should briefly outline your employment history, pointing out specific areas that reflect your ability to handle that particular position. For example, a customer service representative who was looking to upgrade her position to inside sales, emphasized her past responsibilities in a way that showed that even while servicing her clients effectively, she took the extra initiative and expanded her company's sales base by 25%.

This, she explained, resulted in two promotions in five years and a bonus not usually given to customer service representatives.

If you are not familiar with what type of individual the company is looking to hire, you could handle the same question like this:

"If you could tell me more about the job responsibilities, I will be happy to respond based on my background and experience."

It is important to learn the employer's "hot buttons" so you can **sell yourself.** Otherwise, you may go off in an area not even related to what the company is interested in hiring.

NOTE: Some employers give what is called a "negative sell" interview. This interview is geared to screen candidates out - not in! What they are looking for is an individual to overcome all their objections and still appear enthusiastic. Do not let this kind of interview get you down. On the other hand, if the employer has nothing positive to say about the position or the company, you will want to ask quite a few in depth questions to determine if he is just testing you, or really believe this is not a good opportunity.

After listening carefully to the way the employer has described the position, select key words used in the description of the job to relate to your business experience. Remember to interject the employer's name in the conversation from time to time and make sure you pronounce it correctly. Example: "That was a good question, Mary," or, "Mary, you mentioned earlier that your company increased its sales by 23% in 1990, what do you attribute your growth to?"

Attention-getting adjectives to use when preparing your answers:

Positive Attitude	Flexible	Superb	Team Player
Detail Oriented	Creative	Quick Learner	Dedicated
Productive	Independent	Goal Oriented	Motivated
Enthusiastic	Excited	Leader	Efficient

Add more words to your own list to describe yourself. How to incorporate these adjectives into your interview will be discussed later in this chapter. (You can also refer to the list you have compiled for your resume.)

Next, be prepared to answer several tough questions. (I have included solid answers for all of these questions, however, be prepared to improvise and use past experience to back up your answers.) Be sure to use a feature-benefit (see question #7 on page 66) response to every answer. Describe situations by referring to mini-stories (brief summaries) of how you have handled work responsibilities in your current or past positions. Write your response to each question in the blank space provided under each question. This activity will help you when practicing your answers while role playing.

TIP: Always position your questions and answers to show confidence that you will be hired.

Example: "Where will I be sitting" or "When would you need me to start?"

Following are common questions asked by employers and some suggestions for positive answers:

1.)   *Where do you want to be in three to five years?*

_____
_____
_____
_____

Two reasons exist why an employer wants to know the answer to this question:

      a.) How long do you plan to stay with the company?

      b.) How content will you be in this position and for how long?

ANSWER:

"I would like to be with (name of the company) five years from now and be the very best (position title) in your company. I am career oriented and ambitious and after I have proven myself, I would like to know I would be considered for any promotions or opportunities within your firm.

NOTE: If an employer poses a question that catches you off guard or for which you are not prepared, rather than rambling nervously, say: "That is a good question Susan, I would like a moment to think about it." Keep your eyes on the employer and use this time to gather your thoughts. He or she will appreciate your honesty and your answer will appear more sincere.

2.)   *Why should we be interested in hiring you?*

_____
_____
_____
_____
_____
_____
_____
_____

ANSWER:

"The main reason you should hire me is because of my versatility. When I was with XYZ Company, I was in the middle of a major project when our computer system went down. Because the deadline was the next morning, I was able to track down a computer from our sister company, finish the client proposal and go back to the original project I was working on. By the way, not only did we get that account, it was the biggest one in our company's history."

3.)   *Why are you looking for a new position?*

_____
_____
_____
_____
_____
_____

<u>Be cautious when answering this question!</u> Do not be evasive, but steer away from too many negatives.

ANSWER:

"I am searching for a professional company such as yours which will utilize my experience and reward me accordingly. I do not feel my present company can offer this and I am ready to start contributing to an exciting firm like (name of the company)."

4.)   *Does your present employer know you are looking for a new job?*

(Can we check for references?)

_____

_____

_____

_____

_____

ANSWER:

"My present employer is aware that I have been looking for more of a challenge. At this point, I have not informed the company that I am leaving. Please wait until an offer has been made before you check with the company."

5.)   *Why have you made so many job changes?*

_____

_____

_____

_____

_____

If you have made more than two changes in the last five years, **do not be defensive about this question.** Be prepared to answer this confidently and briefly. Do not go into a long explanation. Do not mention money as a prime motivator for leaving, otherwise they will suspect you will do the same to them somewhere down the road.

ANSWER:

"I felt that by joining ABC Company I would enhance its marketing department with my solid analytical background. When the opportunity presented itself to move up in my career with XYZ Company, I had to make a tough decision to leave. All in all, I have learned quite a bit and added a lot to both companies and now am ready to settle down and stay with a company long term."

6.)   ***Why are you interested in our company?***

_____

_____

_____

_____

_____

_____

_____

_____

_____

ANSWER:

"Well, Mary, if you are any indication of your company's staff, than I am most impressed and know we could work well together. Besides, (name of the company) innovative ideas and track record are exciting to me and I am confident I will be an asset and prove creative in this environment."

TIP: This point in the interview is when your homework comes in handy. If you have the opportunity to review the company's annual report in the lobby prior to the interview, use some of that information. Take advantage of this opportunity to flatter the interviewer and the company.

7.) *What are your three greatest strengths?*

_____
_____
_____
_____
_____
_____

*You will want to give a feature/benefit presentation.

ANSWER:

Feature - "My ability to learn quickly."

Benefit - "You will not need to spend your valuable time training me. In fact, my last boss said I was so quick to pick up on my position, he did not even remember training me."

*NOTE: Features describe you or your ability. **Benefits describe what favorable results** they can expect and how you can help solve a company's problems.

8.) *What is your major weakness?*

_____
_____
_____
_____

Everyone has at least one weakness, so do not say you have none. Employers know that no one is perfect. Besides, it is important for you to know where your shortcomings are so you can learn to improve them and work with someone who will compliment your strengths and help you overcome your weaknesses.

ANSWER:

"It is hard for me to relax when I am working on a major project. During my last marketing project, I got so involved that I did not take anytime for myself. Now I spend at least two nights a week relaxing by working out at the health club or reading."

9.)   *Do you have management potential?*

_____
_____
_____
_____
_____

ANSWER:

"Yes, I seem to be a natural leader. Most of my co-workers come to me with a problem because they know I will be able to help them solve it." (Use a **mini-story** to describe a past situation where your leadership or delegating skills were successful.)

If you are more comfortable with a support position rather than management, your answer could be:

"Although I believe I can do most anything that is asked of me, I prefer the role of support or assistant over the managerial role. I excel in anticipating my boss's needs and enjoy the gratification and recognition."

10.)   *Why are you a good manager?*

_____
_____
_____
_____
_____

Site several accomplishments or problem situations which you have handled with business savvy. State reasons why your performance has received attention from top level executives and why your employees respect you. Also mention how your department's profits have increased since you took over and any other financial achievements for which you were responsible.

ANSWER:

"I have a keen eye for hiring excellent employees and helping them to achieve their fullest potential. "In my last position I reduced our department turnover by 50% and 3 of my outside sales representatives were promoted due to their superior performance."

"In fact, our region increased sales from $950,000 to $1,750,000 in just 15 months."

67

11.) *What have you disliked most about past jobs or employers?*

_____
_____
_____
_____
_____

Avoid any NEGATIVE comments. Keep it upbeat and brief.

ANSWER:

"Most of my jobs have been very rewarding. In fact, anything I disliked was minor and I realize there are portions of most positions that are not as glamorous as others. I usually handle the more mundane tasks first, then reward myself with the special projects."

12.) *What do you think you will like best about this job?*

_____
_____
_____
_____
_____

Use the company's words from the job description that was given and expand!!

ANSWER:

"John, you mentioned earlier the commitment XYZ has to team work." "What appeals to me most about this position is the opportunity to interact with all levels of the marketing department on special projects."

13.) *How important is salary to you?*

_____

_____

_____

_____

_____

ANSWER:

"Of course salary is important, however, I am most interested in enjoying what I do and the company I work for. I am sure you are offering a fair salary for the position."

14.) *What have you done in your life or career of which you are most proud?*

_____

_____

_____

_____

List your achievements from Chapter Two that show how well you can handle this position. <u>Paint a vivid picture.</u> Use **action words** to describe what you have accomplished. Be sure to sound excited and enthusiastic when speaking!

ANSWER:

"When I was nominated rookie of the year I certainly was proud of this achievement, however, when I won sales manager of the year I felt this was an even greater accomplishment because it involved motivating an entire team."

15.) *If you had your choice of any job at this moment (dream job) what would it be?*

_____

_____

_____

_____

_____

<u>This can be a trick question.</u> **Do not** tell the interviewer how you would like to own your own company someday. If your answer is not directly related to what the company is offering, you may lose the job offer. Explain how this position meets many of your ideal objectives and that is why you are so excited about the opportunity.

ANSWER:

"Mary, the way you described this position sounds pretty close to my ideal job." "That is why I am so excited about the opportunity to work together."

16.) *What were your best/worst grades in school?*

_____

_____

_____

_____

_____

Emphasize your good grades and how they apply to the position you are seeking. Explain how you have worked on and improved on the subjects in which you did not excel.

ANSWER:

"My English composition classes were certainly a challenge my freshman and sophomore years, yet with a great deal of additional studying I was able to raise my grade to a B+ and I even won a short story contest my senior year." "I maintained a perfect gradepoint average all four years in business math." "I especially enjoyed and excelled in statistics which I realize is a large portion of this position."

17.) *What were the characteristics of your best/worst bosses?*

_____

_____

_____

_____

_____

Be brief with this answer, it could get you into trouble.

ANSWER:

"(Name of the boss) best characteristic were her excellent communication skills. We had mutual respect for each other and I admired her business knowledge. I never had a boss for whom I did not care. Each person has been very different, yet I was able to learn from all of them."

18.) *What are your long and short term goals?*

_____

_____

_____

_____

_____

ANSWER:

"I re-evaluate my short term goals twice a year. This year my major goal is to affiliate myself with a company such as yours and learn all I can about (the industry). My long term goal is to be the best at whatever I do, which may involve continuing my education. My definition of being a success is being a happy and productive person."

TIP: Keep your goals general enough to prevent the company from thinking you are using them as a stepping stone to get to your final destination.

19.) *What will your previous bosses say about you?*

_____
_____
_____
_____
_____

Have a <u>few typed letters of recommendation with you</u> to give to the employer. Be confident anyone you give for a reference is aware you are leaving and will give you a strong recommendation.

ANSWER:

"My last boss said I was the best administrator with whom she has ever worked. In fact, when she learned about me leaving, she offered me another opportunity within the organization."

20.) *If you could change one thing about your present company, what would it be?*

_____
_____
_____
_____
_____

You would not be leaving if it was an ideal place to work, however, if you discuss all the changes you would make, it may seem too aggressive or negative. Play it safe and mention one or two creative ideas that show how innovative you are.

ANSWER:

"I would institute employee brainstorming meetings to gather ideas from those individuals actually performing support roles. This activity would help solve potential problems before they escalate into major ones and would improve employee moral. I would then keep upper management informed on what is happening in the trenches."

21.) *Why were you fired?*

_____

_____

_____

_____

_____

First of all, approach this subject before being asked about it. **(Any red flag areas that you bring up rather than hope they forget will show you are not trying to hide anything.)** Do not get defensive, sad or angry. Just get to the point. Take part of the responsibility; do not blame it all on the company.

ANSWER:

"I was fired because the company and I had different business philosophies. It was a tremendous learning experience. I realized that I can be a success in spite of it and am looking forward to working with a company whose views reflect my own."

22.) *Why should we hire you over the other applicants we have seen?*

_____

_____

_____

_____

_____

ANSWER:

"I feel so strongly about my abilities that if I owned my own company, I would hire someone like myself."

(Again, go into specific reasons why, such as, strengths, achievements, etc.)

23.) *What salary level are you seeking?*

_____
_____
_____
_____
_____

NEVER, NEVER, NEVER quote a figure. I repeat **NEVER, NEVER, NEVER** quote a figure. <u>If you do, you will lose!</u> If you mention a figure too low, you may cheat yourself out of several thousand dollars per year. If you quote too high, the employers might think you are too expensive and hire someone for less money.

ANSWER:

"I would like your best offer. I feel as though I am worth your best offer and I am sure you will be fair."

NOTE: Employers may press you on this subject more than once. Stand firm and tell them that you are negotiable and would appreciate an offer based on your experience. REMEMBER, an employer is using this to feel you out and will often come in low to see how serious you are.

24. *Tell me about a particular crisis and how you handled it. What would you have done differently?*

_____
_____
_____
_____
_____

Recall a time when you took a particularly bad situation and turned it around. Be sure to include what you learned from it and <u>how would you handle it differently in the future.</u>

ANSWER:

"When I first started my position with XYZ I gave a presentation to the Board of Directors. I was not prepared for all the questions they asked. I felt like I had let my staff and my boss down. Now I prepare my presentations extensively to increase my confidence and to ensure that I have all the bases covered!"

25. *Tell me about a successful project you worked on and how it benefitted your company?*

_____
_____
_____
_____

Be specific on this one and do not oversell. If others worked on the project, be sure to include how you worked together as a team to ensure its success.

ANSWER:

"I was part of a team that put on our biggest tradeshow of the year! Being the team leader, I was responsible for tying up all of the loose ends and maintaining our group's motivation. The show was a success and brought in over $750,000 in additional revenue the first two months."

26. *Why have you been out of work for so long?*

_____
_____
_____
_____
_____
_____

<u>Address this question before they do.</u> If you try and hide it or hope they overlook it they will see it as a red flag.

ANSWER:

"Although I have been made several offers during this time, I am not just looking for another paycheck. I am looking for a company where I can really enjoy my work and make a long-term contribution."

NOTE: If you have not had any offers, or if you have been out ill for an extended period of time, emphasize instead what you have learned during your time off and how that can benefit this position. For example, mention how you have learned patience, or how you have learned to budget your finances wisely, etc. Reiterate how being off of work has only made you more enthusiastic for starting a new position!

TIP: Be sure to mention any freelance positions or temporary assignments you have worked on while looking for a full time position. This shows the employer your initiative and flexibility.

27. *Why did you leave your current position without having another lined up?*

_____
_____
_____
_____
_____
_____

If you left on your own accord and were not fired or laid off, the employer may feel you lack responsibility.

ANSWER:

"It was important for me to devote 100% of my energy to my job search and I did not feel it would be fair to my company or myself to keep taking time off work. This way I left on very good terms with them and have had a chance to completely research what I am looking for."

28. *What was your worst failure?*

_____
_____
_____
_____
_____
_____

Be upfront with your answer and recall what a learning experience it has been.

EXAMPLE:

"I once fired an employee who had let an accounting problem get out of hand. I now understand my black and white approach to life was too rigid and am now proactive to their problems rather than reactive."

29. *How would you describe a typical day at your current job?*

_____
_____
_____
_____
_____
_____

Expound on your major responsibilities, but also include the mundane tasks as well. Employers like to see how you roll up your sleeves and pitch in on the less glamorous duties.

ANSWER:

"Due to the nature of my current position each day varies quite a bit, however, my major responsibility of solving customers problems remains constant. I start each day with a follow up plan from the previous day and tackle all the priority items first. I then contact all customers who need additional information on our product and either take their order or refer them to an appropriate salesperson. If all my work is current I offer my assistance to the credit or sales departments."

30.   *How do you feel about working overtime?*

_____
_____
_____
_____
_____

You want to tell them that you are always willing to put in the extra effort a certain project requires. Yet also, let them know that because of your efficiency you have been able to complete your work for the most part in a regular work week. **You should always find out how much overtime is typical and is it expected of you.**

ANSWER:

"I realize to meet deadlines or while working on special projects, overtime is necessary and I am quite willing to do what is needed." "I also am quite active outside the office and participate in many activities." "How often is my overtime expected?"

STOP! Before you answer the last question, <u>have you taken the time to actually fill in the blanks with your own answers</u>? Or do you think you will remember all your answers and it isn't necessary to write them down.? <u>Writing down the answers will serve you two ways</u>. First, it will clarify in your mind what you really want to say and secondly, writing your answers will firmly ingrain them in your mind. **Being prepared with written answers prior to the interview will give you extra confidence and peace of mind during the actual interview.**

31.) *Do you have any more questions?*

_____
_____
_____
_____
_____
_____

YES, YES, YES, YES, YES, YES, YES, YES, YES, YES. **If your answer is no, you are not interested in the job offer.** Answering yes shows your intelligence, enthusiasm, and that you have been listening.

ANSWER:

"Yes, do you feel my qualifications and experience are what you are looking for? I certainly hope so because I am very interested in the position and having an opportunity to work with you."

The employer wants to know how interested you are before he/she takes more time to explain about the company, etc. **Intelligent questions can seal the job offer for you.** Read on for 15 ideal questions to ask the employer in order to learn more about him and help you decide if this is the right company and position for you.

TIP: Body language and eye contact play a crucial role in convincing an employer of your honesty and confidence level. Sit upright toward the edge of your seat (as if you are ready and anxious to start working). **You must look the employer in the eyes the entire interview!** Even if the employer is not always looking at you. This is especially important when the employer has asked you a question such as "what is your greatest strength?" If you have a hard time looking directly in the employer's eyes, look at his forehead (it will appear as though you are maintaining eye contact).

QUESTIONS YOU CAN ASK THE HIRING OFFICIAL

1.) What specifically do you need me to accomplish in the first 90 days?

2.) How long have you been with the company?

3.) What do you like best about working here?*

4.) What are the company goals for the next five years?

5.) How is success measured in this corporation? (Ask to see an organizational chart)

6.) What is the best track record of (title of position you are applying for)?

7.) Who are your major competitors?

8.) Why is this position open?

9.) What are the prior problem areas in this position?

10.) What has been your growth rate throughout the past five years? How does it compare to the industry growth rate?

11.) Where is the company headquartered and where (if any) are the offices located?

12.) What is the first thing you need me to do to reduce your workload?

13.) How does my background and experience compare to others that you have interviewed?

14.) Where do you see this position leading over the next two to three years?

15.) Would you consider me for this position?

TIP: If you are not sure you want the position, keep interviewing as though you are. You can always turn down the offer. Besides, the employers may be so impressed they will revamp the position to interest you. The employer may even have something else in mind for you elsewhere in the company.

ALWAYS INTERVIEW TO GET THE JOB OFFER!

---

*NOTE: (Question number 3 will give you the chance to get to know the employer on a more personal basis. This information is important in developing rapport.)

DO NOT (at this time) ask about salary, benefits or personnel policies. You want to appear achievement oriented, not only interested in what they have to offer. Once the offer is made you can ask all about the extra perks of the job. Even if the information is not volunteered during the interview, be patient. **Wait until you have been made an offer to inquire about salary, benefits, vacation time, etc.**

If the employer makes you an offer on the spot, ask for 24 hours to review all the information you have gathered. Often in our excitement we readily accept the offer, only to find ourselves wondering if we did the right thing. Most employers will have no problem giving you at least one day to think it over. However, if you ask for a week to decide, many will assume you are not interested and continue their interviewing process. Remember, the offer is not final until you have accepted. An employer may want to offer the position to someone else if you ask for more than one or two days to decide.

The last few minutes of the interview are very critical. Thank them for the time they have spent, reiterate how very interested you are and ask them when you can expect to hear from them.

If the employer does not summarize the interview or process for you, ask him to provide a summary. If you have another offer pending, now is the time to let the employer know about it. This will either help him make his decision quickly about hiring you, or the employer may encourage you not to let your other offer slip away. At least you will know where you stand. (One unique benefit to using an employment service is immediate feedback from the employer on your chances.)

Leave the interview on an upbeat note. **Tell the employer you are looking forward to hearing from him and working together.** This response will show your enthusiasm and confidence. If you have not already seen the facilities, ask for a brief tour. Some employers automatically incorporate this into the interview, some only reserve a tour for those in whom they are interested. If the employer seems rather hurried or they have another appointment waiting, do not prolong it. He may get irritated. However, if he seems to be enjoying talking with you and appears interested in you, say something like, "You have very nice offices here, would you mind showing me around?"

Once you get back to your car, spend a minute or two to write down any questions or thoughts about the interview. First impressions are good indicators when making your final decision.

If you have no other appointments that day and are interested in pursuing this opportunity, then it is time to go to the next step, the thank you letter.

> **TIP:** Make sure to get the interviewer's business card for the exact title and spelling of his name (for the thank you letter).

chapter
seven

Creative
Follow up
That
GETS YOU HIRED

FOLLOW UP

Following up after the interview is AS IMPORTANT as preparing for one.

Immediately following the interview, write a thank you letter.

Following are two examples that present the proper thank you letter format.

Sample thank you letter #1.

Date

(Employers Address)

Dear (Name):

Thank you for taking the time from your busy schedule on (day) to discuss the (position/title) currently available with (name of company).

Your insight into this position was both refreshing and exciting to me!

As we discussed, my experience and success in my previous positions have prepared me to meet the challenge of excelling in the role of Administrative Assistant to the President, Ms. Jill Halper.

I am confident that when given the opportunity to demonstrate my strong organizational ability and excellent people skills, I would make a valuable contribution to (name of company).

Thank you again for your courtesy. It was a pleasure to meet you and learn more about your firm.

I look forward to hearing from you soon and seeing you again in the near future.

Sincerely,

Name

Sometimes an interviewer introduces you to another person who becomes part of the meeting. **Following is an example of a proper note to that individual.**

Sample Thank you Letter #2

Date

(Employer's Address)

Dear (Name):

It was a pleasure meeting you today when I was at (company name) to interview with (name of employer) for the job of (position).

The description you gave of your program sounds very much like the program I helped Corporate Image solve when I worked there last summer as a systems intern. Your remarks about the casual, friendly atmosphere you enjoy at (company name) made me feel very much at home.

Again, I did appreciate the opportunity to talk with you and hope that we will be working together in the near future.

Sincerely,

Name

> **NOTE:** I cannot stress enough the importance of a well-written thank you letter. **Send one to each person you interview with and each time you go back** (whether it be a second, third or even fourth interview). Use your creativity and imagination to write something different each and every time!

Be creative, yet professional. Make sure the letter reflects your "style" as your resume did. **When composing the letter, be sure to overcome any objections the employer may have had during the interview and include any areas that might not have been covered.** Briefly summarize again why you would be the best candidate for the position and end the letter on a confident note.

Thank you letters should be typed. If that is not possible, a neatly handwritten note on a professional white card or a business thank you card can be substituted. The content is **very** important and just as crucial is correct spelling, punctuation and grammar.

> **TIP:** Remember to refer to your interviewer's business card for the correct spelling of his name. Several situations have been noted of candidates losing job offers because they spelled the hiring official or company name wrong.

The letter should be sent the same day as you interviewed! **Better yet, hand deliver it to the company.** This shows your promptness and enthusiasm.

One alternative to a conservative thank you letter is the creative thank you response.

The impact you make with some creativeness can get you the job offer or at least a second interview. Any doubts the interviewers might have had may be overlooked by your fresh approach.

It is important for you to gather a sense of the employer's personality to decide whether a conservative thank you letter, telegram or creative thank you will be more effective.

To help assist you in making your decision on which approach to use **take note of the following success stories resulting over the years.**

Success Stories From Creative Thank Yous

---

*N*ever underestimate the value of a dollar. One candidate who knew she was in second place after the final interview, felt she had nothing to lose and everything to gain by being daring. She wrote a confident thank you note and included a crisp one dollar bill. In the letter she stated she would bet the company one dollar that she could do a better job than candidate number one. The employers took her up on her offer and were thrilled with her moxie. No one knows what happened to candidate number one.

*A*n incident well-remembered involved another second place contender. She took the opportunity to WOW a leading soft drink company by sending a single rose in one of the company's empty pop bottles. Not only did the employers find her clever and creative, they felt with her charm she could knock the socks off their clients. **They hired her the very same day.**

*O*ne candidate used the old cliche, "a way to a person's heart is through his stomach." The company is a well known pizza firm. This innovative person wanted to convince the hiring authority of her enthusiasm. She had one of their pizzas delivered to his office for lunch with a note that read, "This is my first investment in your company." Needless to say, she has been happily employed and enjoying that company's pizza ever since.

*A*nother candidate whose accounting skills were not quite what this company required sent a telegram that read, "Add (+) me to your <u>payroll</u> and I will be a <u>credit.</u>. Anyone else would be a <u>debit</u>." Convinced that at least he knew the right terminology and was quite innovative, the company took a risk and hired him. Six months later, the hiring authority said that he was the best accounting clerk in the department.

A favorite recollection is when a personal friend was trying to break into the real estate field. Without having previous industry experience, she found herself competing with individuals who had "stronger" backgrounds. Feeling that her initial interview with a prominent home builder went quite well, she wanted to ensure her chances of getting a job offer. She wanted to knock his socks off with a dynamic thank you letter. What she did took both creativity and moxie. She purchased a SOLD sign from a local office supply store and had them engrave the company's name with whom she wanted the job. In the blank area she wrote, **You've sold me on ABC Company.** Later that day she hand delivered the sign to the employer's office. Now, how could he not have offered her the job? Well, he did not. Here is why.

After dropping off the sign, she went home to wait for his call. It never came. By the following day she was concerned he had not personally received it. As the day slipped by, she still had not heard anything. What if he thought it was a stupid idea? As her thoughts grew more and more negative, she decided to give up on the whole thing. She did not call him.

Several months passed and she had by now accepted a position with a smaller firm. One day while she was manning the sales desk, in walked the hiring manager who she had delivered the sign to. Curious about why she had never heard from him, she mustered up all her courage and asked him why he never called her. In a very excited manner he said, "That was the most creative and impressive thank you I ever received, if you had called me back I would have hired you on the spot."

The moral of this story is: **"Go after what you want 100%!"** Do not let your fear stand in the way of your success.

All that fear means is:

False
Expectations
Appearing
Real

The same energy is used in fear as in excitement. It is just directed differently!

One client interviewed two candidates for the same position. Equally impressed he had a hard decision to make. Who should he choose? What he did is not an uncommon occurrence. He hired them both! One for an Administrative Assistant position and the other candidate for a Marketing Support Representative. Something the second candidate did really stood out. The firm that hired her was a national pager company. Knowing that the hiring official was leaving town for a week, after her initial interview, she knew she would not be able to get him a thank you letter the next day. By using his pager number she was able to leave him a detailed voice mail message thanking him for the interview and stating how excited she was to meet him and was anxious to try out his product.

NOTE: After the thank you note, card, letter or telegram has been sent or delivered, wait one to two days to insure its receipt and telephone the employer. Chances are, if you sent a telegram or other delivery, you probably have already received a call (most likely with an offer!).

When you are following up by telephone, be enthusiastic! Do not be put off by unanswered calls. Remember, **patience, tenacity and a positive outlook** are crucial in convincing an employer to make you the offer.

TIP: Do not leave a message! Always tell the receptionist you will be happy to call back. This way, the employer will not return your call when you are:

    A.   Getting out of the shower

    B.   Eating (with your mouth full)

    C.   Sleeping

    D.   Out for the day

    E.   Unprepared

NOTE: If you do not already have an answering machine, I suggest buying one. You may lose an interview or offer by not being available to get the call or message. Be sure to leave a professional sounding message!

The Decision Finally:

The employer calls you and gives you the news you want to hear: **"Congratulations and welcome aboard. You have got the job!"** Great! Now comes the fun part, negotiating your salary and compensation package. (see Chapter Eight)

If by chance the company made a mistake and chose someone else for the position, take a deep breath, relax and reread chapters Two and Five. Critique yourself on your interview. If you were qualified for the position, ask yourself on what you could have improved and you can do differently the next time around? **(Call the employer and ask why he chose another person.)** Ask him to be direct so the answer (information) can help you in the future.)

If the company sends you a formal rejection letter, it is still beneficial for you to call and find out why the employer went with another candidate and not yourself. Listen carefully and take notes.

Here are a few questions you should ask the employer in the case of rejection:

1. *How could I better present myself and my background in the future?*

2. *What qualifications or characteristics did the person you hire have that I lacked?*

3. *Will you consider me for another opportunity with your firm? If yes, when do you foresee a position opening?*

chapter eight

YOU'RE HIRED...
Negotiate a WIN-WIN Agreement

Great, so you got the job offer! Now, do not get so excited that you accept it without some thorough thought. **The process of deciding whether or not you will accept the company's offer should begin during the initial interview.** This way, you will be prepared when the offer is made. Usually the offer is given over the telephone. However, it is just as common for the employer to invite you back to make the offer in person.

When the offer is made on the telephone, get your notes out and ask any questions that remain unanswered. Make sure you get specific. For Example: benefit coverage - how much is your contribution? When does the coverage begin?)

The following are questions that should be answered before a job offer is accepted.

SALARY:

1.)   Gross annual salary. (Not net salary)

2.)   When are you eligible for an increase? Are the increases based on performance or are they given company-wide?

3.)   How much is a typical raise for this position? (Merit or cost of living)

INSURANCE:

1.)   Full explanation of hospitalization and major medical, dental and vision if provided.

2.)   What portion (if any) are you responsible for? (single or family coverage)

3.)   What is the deductible?

4.)   When do the benefits go into effect?

5.)   Is pension, profit sharing or the 401K plan offered? (Employer paid?)

6.)   Is it an HMO or a PPO?

7.)   If you elect not to take the company's insurance, can you take the amount the company would normally contribute and add that to your salary?

HOURS:

1.) Is this a salaried or hourly position?

2.) What are your normal working hours?

3.) Is overtime expected? (If so, are you paid for it?)

4.) If it is a salaried position and overtime is necessary, do you receive compensation time?

VACATION:

1.) When are you eligible?

2.) How much time is allotted?

3.) If you do not take it will it be forfeited? Does it carry over or can you be paid for it?

BONUS:

1.) Is there a performance-based bonus? One based on company profits? A Christmas bonus?

REVIEWS:

1.) How often will you be reviewed? Is it monetary?

SALES POSITIONS:

1.) Base salary? Draw vs. commission?* Straight commission? Incentives? Bonus? Expense reimbursement? Company car/car allowance? When are commissions paid?

*NOTE: If you take a draw salary, will you have to pay it back if you leave the company?

Having this knowledge will help you in making an educated decision regarding accepting an offer.

If you are still hesitant about accepting the offer, inform the employer that you are definitely interested in his offer and that you will review all this information and give him your answer the following day (within 24 hours). He may give you the weekend or a couple of days. Do not ask for any longer time period. If you ask for a week, this will show the employer you have some hesitations and are probably not interested in joining his team. If you wait too long to accept, the employer has the right to keep interviewing and may extend the job offer to another candidate.

Once you have gathered all the information necessary, create a PROs and CONs list to help you make a good decision!

PRO	CON
$5,000 salary increase	One hour travel (longer in bad weather)
Opportunity to learn new computer system	Company has had several management changes recently (How stable are they?)

Go through your list thoroughly until you are completely satisfied that you have covered everything. Add up your PROs and then your CONs. **Whichever column is greater is the decision you need to go with.** Do not try and talk yourself in another direction. Make your decision based on both your intuition as well as the results of your list. Use good common sense. For example, do not accept an offer if you do not care for the person for whom you will be working even if the position is paying a great deal more money. Chances are, you will be miserable and the extra money will not be worth it.

This decision is yours and yours alone. It is great to have input from others, however, your spouse, friend, relative, etc., <u>is not the person who will be working there.</u> However, if travel or relocation is involved, it should be a family decision.

Throughout the years, many situations have required attention regarding salary negotiation. <u>When going through an agency, it is always best to let your account executive handle the salary negotiations.</u> Recruiters are trained to be an objective third party negotiator which can usually result in a higher starting salary.

If you do not have the benefit of someone working on your behalf, you can certainly **negotiate for yourself.** For instance, the company has just offered you the position for $2,000 less than for what you had hoped. After thanking the company for the offer, tell the employers you are very interested and would like some time to make your decision. Explain that you will call them the following day to let them know your decision.

The following day your telephone conversation could go something like this:

"Thank you (hiring official's name) for offering me the opportunity to work for (name of the company). I have given the position you offered me a great deal of thought and am excited to come to work with you, however, I have one concern. You have made me a fair salary offer yet I have had a chance to review what this position entails and really believe I can do a great job, however, I was looking for a higher salary and would appreciate you reconsidering my salary offer." (Keep silent and let them think.)

The employer may not have the authority to make this decision or may want some time to think about it. <u>You will also have to decide, if they cannot go any higher, will you take the position anyway?</u> If the employer responds by saying "I am sorry, but that is the highest we can pay right now." Respond by saying, **"Is it possible to review me after three months instead of the standard six-month or yearly review? At that time, once I have proven myself, would I be eligible for an increase?"** (<u>Make sure that if they agree to an increase after three or six months, it will not affect your raise on your one-year anniversary</u>.) **Many people fear losing the offer if they try and negotiate a higher salary than the employer offered. If any employer would get angry over something like this, would you really want to work for him? What will it be like at raise time every year?** Remember, you are worth the best offer and more, **DO NOT SETTLE FOR LESS!** Keep in mind however, that <u>you need to be realistic.</u> Asking for $5,000 more than the marketplace is paying is not a wise idea.

Once you have decided to accept the position, I suggest you request your offer and compensation package be put in writing.

If your position requires a contract, check with your attorney **before signing anything.**

chapter nine

STARTING a NEW JOB with CONFIDENCE

The time has come to do the dreaded deed, giving your resignation. Maybe in your case you cannot wait to sing the song, "Take this job and ...."

This is the time to exhibit a great deal of willpower. Whatever your opinion is of the company that you are leaving, it is very **important not to burn your bridges**. You may need the company for a reference down the road.

First, write or type a resignation letter to your immediate boss, carbon copy to personnel. **Make sure you notify them before you start celebrating with your co-workers.**

Some companies ask for exit interviews. (This procedure gives them the opportunity to learn what their mistakes were.) Be honest during this meeting, yet do not jump on the bandwagon and create animosity. It is very important to be courteous and professional during this time, as emotions tend to run high for all involved.

THE PROPER NOTICE FOR MOST POSITIONS IS AS FOLLOWS:	
Under One Year	One Week
One to Two Years	One to Two Weeks
Two to Five Years	Two to Three Weeks
Five Years	Three Weeks to One Month

As soon as you give your resignation, request your letter of recommendation. It is important to receive it right away. As time goes on, you risk having the employer take your resignation personally. Especially if he counteroffers you and you do not accept.

It is strongly suggested to not even contemplate accepting a counteroffer.

Five reasons to NEVER accept a counteroffer.

1.) Having once demonstrated your lack of loyalty, your absences or time off will always be questioned.

2.) Many times, counteroffers are an employer's way of stalling until he can replace you. (At his convenience.)

3.) Will you have to threaten to quit every time you want a raise or the promotion you deserve?

4.) What is really going to change? Even if the employer does give you more money or another title--is his attitude that made you look elsewhere going to change as well?

5.) Where is this new-found money coming from for your raise? Is it your next increase given early?

A few exceptions will always exist when counteroffers have proven to work out beautifully, however, the majority of individuals who accept them end up leaving the company within one year.

During the time after you have given notice to when you leave your company, it is important to keep your desk and job responsibilities up to date. Do not use this time to goof off and play. Help train your replacement. If possible, leave detailed notes for the new person to make his or her transition easier. **The more organized and professional your departure is, the more fondly you will be remembered come reference time and remember, you too are starting a new position and would like the same courtesy.**

Okay, it is your first day on the new job. Dress as you did on your first interview. You will soon learn the dress code and what is and is not acceptable. (No matter what your position, it is always best to dress your absolute best at all times -- even if you have not "made it" yet,

always dress as though you have.) **When you invest in a smart business wardrobe, you are investing in yourself.**

By all means, take the initiative and introduce yourself to your coworkers. Yes, it is understandable that you may be nervous, yet if you wait for the other employees to seek you out, you may wait a long time. Being quiet or shy can be perceived as being unfriendly or distant.

Leave your lunch at home the first day and ask a coworker to join you. Better yet, your new boss may invite you out for a get acquainted lunch.

If your company has no formal company tour, **take some time and get familiar with your new surroundings.** It will make you feel more at home and build your confidence to know where everything is located.

Most firms have some sort of training, although some still use the old "sink or swim" type training programs. Whatever your case, make sure you take notes. Nothing is more irritating than to have to answer the same question over and over again. It also makes you look like a slow learner.

Take initiative and ask questions. If you are not clear about something, it is better to ask than to guess incorrectly and have to do it all again. Ask thoughtful questions pertaining to the position. Solid questions may give you an added edge. In fact, if you are catching on very quickly and are anxious to jump ahead, inform the person who is training you that he is doing such a good job at explaining things you are ready for the next step. If you find yourself overwhelmed or falling behind, ask the individual to slow down a bit. Offer to stay late or come in early for additional training. (Or get materials that can be taken home to study.) Try not to overburden your coworkers with too many questions, after all, they have their jobs to do as well

and may become resentful. In fact, if you find yourself receiving a good deal of help from a coworker, offer to take him out to lunch or for a drink for all his assistance.

Give yourself about a month to get acclimated. By this time, everything will start to sink in and you will find your confidence starting to build.

If your new employer does not suggest a 30 day review, ask him to sit down with you and go over the areas in which you may need to improve. This is a learning time. Do not expect your employers to tell you how great you are progressing (even if you are). Focus more on what you need to learn to perform better in your position. Rely on yourself to provide the compliments you deserve. Otherwise, you may be disappointed and a bit resentful. Keep a positive attitude and give your new position your best effort.

Remember, by completing this book and taking action on what you've learned, you have already distinguished yourself as a person who is prepared and on the road to a new and exciting career!

Good Luck And Best Wishes For Continued Success,
Vicki Spina

<u>*POSTSCRIPT:*</u>   *Searching for a new position can be frustrating and lonely at times, to say the least. Many of the candidates that I have assisted through the years, felt as though I was their coach. <u>Why not ask one of your friends or family to use this book along with you and be your coach</u>? After all, anything done with another as support, will help your job search become much more enjoyable and rewarding!*

If we all work together, we can make the world as one.

ABOUT THE AUTHOR....

Vicki Spina's knowledge of innovative interviewing techniques stem from her 13 year successful track record in the employment industry. In her rookie year, Ms. Spina earned the award of Account Executive in the Nation and was also named the Midwest Account Executive of the Year. Ms. Spina owns Corporate Image, an employment consulting service in the Chicago area and instructs seminars based on her book GETTING HIRED IN THE '90s. Several excerpts of her book and articles pertaining to employment issues are currently being published in leading magazines. Spina's dynamic style is showcased in her speaking engagements, consulting practice and in her teaching to area colleges and organizations.

For information regarding Ms. Spina's consulting services and seminars please write **Corporate Image Consulting 1450 E. American Ln. Ste. 1400 Schaumburg, IL 60173 or call (708) 330-4433**

Consulting services are available over the telephone or in person. Resume critiques, consultations or preparation can be completed via mail, fax or in person. Please feel free to call Vicki directly for details on all services that she offers.

In addition, Ms. Spina volunteers her time to Global Relationship seminars, which is dedicated to World Peace and she is actively involved in community services to improve unemployment.

INDEX

DID YOU **BORROW** THIS **COPY OF**
GETTING HIRED IN THE '90s?

If so, now is the time to order YOUR OWN personal copy so you can refer to it as often as you like!

_____ YES, I am interested in receiving the most up-to-date job search information available! RUSH me _____ copies of "Getting Hired In The '90s" at $14.95 plus $5.00 per book to cover postage and handling charges.

_____

Ordered By: _____   **Ship To:** _____

_____   _____

_____   _____

Daytime Phone: (   )_____

100% MONEY BACK GUARANTEE

If after using the ideas
presented in this book,
you have not received a job
offer in 90 Days, write to
Corporate Image Publishers
for a 100% refund.

SAVE 20% on orders of 4 or more copies.
Discount_____

MAKE CHECKS OR MONEY ORDERS

PAYABLE TO:
Corporate Image
1450 E. American Ln.
Suite 1400
Schaumburg, IL 60173
Or Call: **(708) 330-4433**

Quantity Ordered_____
Shipping & Handling_____
Subtotal_____
AMT.ENCLOSED_____
(IL RESIDENTS ADD 8% SALES TAX)

TO CHARGE BY PHONE CALL
1-800.247-6553

PHONE ORDERS CAN BE BILLED TO ANY MAJOR CREDIT CARD

GETTING HIRED IN THE '90s

CANDIDATE DATABASE

Getting Hired in the '90s now offers *kiNexus*, the nation's largest and fastest growing database of candidates seeking employment.

Whether you are currently employed or in the process of a career search, *kiNexus* membership enables you to network (confidentially if you wish) with thousands of companies -- ranging from Fortune 500s to medium-sized and smaller companies -- with actual positions to fill. Companies nationwide are tapping into the kiNexus database every day because they know it is both a more cost-effective and efficient way for them to find the right candidates.

You may now register in the *kiNexus* database for a fee of $30.00. A confirmation and a representative sample listing of current corporate subscribers will be sent to you upon receipt of your registration form. Your resume will remain in the database for one year during which you may update it at any time. As an added benefit, first time registrants will also receive a complementary issue of the **Career Network Job Bulletin**, a newsletter which contains hundreds of job openings throughout the country.

To register, simply complete the information below and return it with an attached resume and payment of $30.00 to the *kiNexus* National Data Center, at 640 North LaSalle Street, Suite 560, Chicago, IL, 60610.

REGISTRATION FORM   -   REGISTRATION FORM   -   REGISTRATION FORM   -   REGISTRATION FORM   -

---

Enter your desired career and industry preferences.

ie. Systems Director in the Health Care Industry.

Enter the career and industry that you have experience in and the duration of that experience.

ie. Computer Programmer in the Financial Services Industry.

Name:_____

Desired Career Fields: _____   _____

Desired Industry Fields: _____   _____

Are you willing to relocate: Yes   No

If yes, please circle up to two geographic preferences:

Northeast Southeast Midwest Northwest West Southwest International Any

Primary Career Experience: _____   _____

Primary Industry Experience: _____   _____

Length of Primary Experience:_____/_____   _____/_____
　　　　　　　　　　　　　　　Year(s)/Month(s)   　Year(s)/Month(s)

I agree that kiNexus may release the information I have provided via the kiNexus Career Network to recruiting employers.

Signature: _____Date:_____

Registration Fees

If paying by credit card, be sure to provide both the card number and expiration date.

Please do not send cash.

□Candidate Registration $30   □Confidential Registration $50 (we will contact you prior to releasing your name, address and phone number.)

□Check or Money Order payable to Information Kinetics

Credit Card No._____   Exp: Mo_____   Yr_____

Signature_____   Date_____

---

640 North LaSalle · Suite 560 · Chicago, Illinois · 60610 · 800-828-0422 · Fax 312-642-0616